W9-AYR-595

"Each second we live is a new and unique moment of the universe, a moment that will never be again... And what do we teach our children? We teach them that two and two make four and that Paris is the capital of France.

When will we also teach them: do you know who you are? You are a marvel. You are unique. In all the years that have passed, there has never been another child like you. And look at your body – what a wonder it is! Your legs, your arms, your clever fingers, the way you move. You may become a Shakespeare, a Michelangelo, a Beethoven. You have the capacity for anything. Yes, you are a marvel. And when you grow up, can you then harm another who is, like you, a marvel? You must cherish one another. You must work – we must all work – to make this world worthy of its children."

Pablo Casals

A famous Spanish musician, also noted for his humanitarian beliefs.

(1876 - 1973)

I'm Hip-hop, the rapping rabbit from a
starship far away,
It looks so good down here on Earth,
I think I'm going to stay.
I just love this planet and you human
beings too,
And I've bounced across five galaxies
to have a word with you...

LIFE EDUCATION

I Am Special

Written by
Alexandra Parsons

Illustrated by
Ann Johns, John Shackell, and Stuart Harrison

FRANKLIN WATTS
A Division of Grolier Publishing
LONDON • NEW YORK • HONG KONG • SYDNEY
DANBURY, CONNECTICUT

8944191

© Franklin Watts 1996
Text © Life Education/Franklin Watts

First American Edition 1997 by
Franklin Watts
A Division of Grolier Publishing
Sherman Turnpike
Danbury, Connecticut 06816

Parsons, Alexandra.
   I am special / Alexandra Parsons. -- 1st
    American ed. p. cm. -- (Life education)
   Includes index.
   Summary: Examines the various ways of being
an individual, discussing the forming of
opinions, friendships, teamwork, competition,
and dealing with feelings and differences.
   ISBN 0-531-14421-6
   1. Individuality in children--Juvenile literature.
[1. Individuality.] I. Title. II. Series.
BF723.I56P37 1997
155.4'182--dc20   96-2136 CIP AC

10 9 8 7 6 5 4 3 2 1

Edited by: Helen Lanz
Designed by: Sally Boothroyd
Commissioned photography by:
Peter Millard
Illustrations by: Ann Johns,
John Shackell, and Stuart Harrison

Printed in Italy

Acknowledgments:
Commissioned photography by Peter Millard:
10, 12 (all),15, 17, 18.
Researched photography: Popperfoto; 23.
Artwork: all cartoons of "alien" by Stuart
Harrison. Other cartoon illustrations by
Ann Johns: cover, title page, 8, 9, 13 (bottom),
16-17, 22: John Shackell: contents page, 11, 13
(top), 14-15, 20-21, 23, 24-25. Timeline by
Oliver Jones: 18-19.

Franklin Watts and Life Education International
are indebted to Vince Hatton and Laurie Noffs
for their invaluable help.

Franklin Watts would like to extend their special
thanks to all the actors who appear in the Life
Education books:

Calum Heath   Jade Hoffman
Frances Lander   Karamdeep Sandhar

Contents

What makes me special? . .

There is no one else like you in the whole wide world. Not one single person. You do not look exactly the same as any other person (unless you are an identical twin!), and you do not think and feel the same things as your friends or family. That makes you very special.

Other people are special too

There is no way of telling what people are like inside just by looking at them. You can't say, for instance, that people with red hair are all bad-tempered or that they all like carrots.

You simply have no way of guessing what people are like until you get to know them.

Which of these children do you think you could make friends with? It is difficult to tell just by looking at them, isn't it?

What makes a person special?

Before you can make up your mind about others, you need to know a bit about their personalities. It would be helpful to know if they are quiet or lively, funny or serious, show-offs or shy. These children now give you a little more help by wearing their own clothes and telling you something about themselves:

My name is Melanie. I'm a bit shy with people I don't know very well. When I'm by myself, I like listening to music. I want to be a dancer when I grow up.

My name is Dora. Most people think I need helping all the time, but I don't. I just can't walk, that's all. I like relaxed people who laugh a lot, just like me! I want to be a comedian or a cartoonist.

Hi, I'm Joe. I hate being cooped up inside the house. I love all kinds of sports. I want to be a parachutist or a soccer player.

My name is Grace. Some people say I talk too much, but I've got so much to say! I love writing stories. I love math and science. I want to be a doctor – like my mom and dad.

Some of you are funny, some of you are zany,

Some of you are moody, and some of you are brainy.

But each of you is precious, you see,

Because you're the only you that will ever be!

9

Me by me . . . .

What kind of a person are YOU? Are you quiet or noisy? Are you sporty? Are you clever? Are you silly?

Think of some words to describe what you are like. Then ask a friend to find words to describe you. Don't be offended — no one is perfect! Friends may see you in a different way, so it could be interesting to compare their list of words with yours.

Here are some words to help you
See if you can think up some more.

Athletic
Brainy
Creative
Daring
Energetic
Friendly
Gentle
Happy
Independent

Jolly
Kind
Lively
Moody
Noisy
Outgoing
Peaceful
Quiet
Reliable

Serious
Thoughtful
Understanding
Vain
Wonderful
X-ceptional!
a Yo-yo
Zany

Drawing a self portrait

Sit down with a piece of paper, a pencil, and a mirror. Look at yourself in the mirror for a moment.

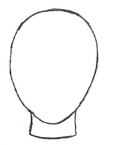

1. Now draw the shape of your face and neck. Don't make the neck too thin.

2. Now mark in the position of your eyes, just roughly. Not too high!

3. Mark the position of your nose and mouth.

4. And now sketch in your ears, hair, and eyebrows.

5. Think about the expression you are going to put on your face. Are you going to make your eyes wide open and your mouth and cheeks all smiley?

6. You may want to go for the thoughtful look.

I look in the mirror, and I know what I see —

That person looking back at me is me!

Sometimes I'm sad, but mostly I'm happy,

So smile back at me, and make it snappy!

7. Or something a little out of the ordinary...

8. Now you can fill in all the details.

9. And give yourself a bit of color.

It's a one-of-a-kind masterpiece. Just like you!

My feelings . . . .

Feelings can be hurt – just like knees can get scraped and toes can get stepped on. But mending hurt feelings often takes a lot more than a bandage.

A

B

Showing feelings

Feelings are for sharing. Think of all the different ways you can show how you feel. Look at these faces and see if you can match them up with the feelings listed below:

Angry
Sad
Happy
Proud
Frightened
Thrilled

C

D

Feeling bad

Sometimes very sad things happen; it is part of life. Parents may split up, someone you love may get very sick, friends may move away, or a pet may die. People often get angry with everybody when they feel sad inside. It is a good thing to be able to talk to somebody about why you feel sad.

E

F

What's the matter with Joe?

Feeling good

Happy feelings are much more fun. You can feel wonderful and excited about a treat, or you can feel good about yourself because you've achieved something. Making other people happy is a pretty good feeling too.

Happy feelings are good to share.

It's great to know that people care.

And when you're sad and feelin' blue,

Talk to your friends – they'll listen to you!

Two ways to feel happy

My friends . . . .

Why do you like your friends? Probably because they make you feel relaxed and happy, and you like doing the same things. Good friends like each other just the way they are. They don't want to make them do things they don't want to do.

My friend Toby

Mom, Toby's invited me to his house after school tomorrow. Can I go?

Who's Toby?

Oh he's a new boy. He's really cool, Mom. Everyone wants to be friends with him. And he wants to be friends with me.

That's nice.

There's nothing to do. This neighborhood stinks.

We could go bug hunting. That's mega-good fun... or build a den in the garden...

Oh, bugs, how thrilling! How about we give that old man who lives on the corner a bit of a scare.

Well, I... I don't think that would be very nice.

Come on! You look like the kind of guy who's got what it takes to be daring and different.

We've got the great bug hunt this afternoon, and Mom's bringing this big picnic. It'll be great.

It's too tame for me. I'm going to play with my new friend Toby.

Oh! But we've planned this for ages... You're the best bug hunter in the universe... I wish you'd come.

How can you tell
who's a real friend?

Someone who'll stick with you
to the end.

Real friends know
how to give and take.

A friend who wants to change
you is a no-good fake.

My ideas . . . .

Where do your ideas come from? They come from your experiences in life. You get ideas from listening to your friends and your family, and adding a little something of your own. Often friends and family members have different ideas about things.

What is an opinion?

Having an opinion means making up your mind about something or someone. It is wise to think for a bit before forming an opinion, and it is important that your opinions are your own, not someone else's! It is good to talk about opinions. It helps you decide what you really think, and you may even change your mind.

A good discussion helps everyone make up their minds ...

I think people worry too much about animals and not enough about people.

Animals have rights. We have a lot to learn from animals. I'm a vegetarian.

But you eat fish, and fish are animals. And you eat eggs, and eggs might grow up to be animals.

Shut up!

Animals eat each other. Has someone told spiders not to eat flies? Or owls not to eat mice? Or big fish not to eat little fish? Why shouldn't we do what the animals do?

I like meat. If nobody ate meat, what would happen to farms? What would farmers do? What would happen to all the pigs and lambs and cows and chickens? Who would be bothered to look after them?

What do you think, Sally?

I think it's OK to eat meat as long as the animals have had a nice life and have been properly looked after.

BEWARE! Some people have opinions just because it suits what they want...

You think one way, I think another.

My opinions aren't my brother's.

Think through all the ideas and facts

before you decide what's this and what's that.

I think the playground should be turned into a soccer field.

I think the playground should be turned into a garden.

I think that different people want to use the playground in different ways. It isn't fair to make the whole playground suit just one group. I think we should make different areas.

My memories . . . .

Can you tell the story of your life so far? Some people have better memories than others, but you can always get help from family and friends to fill in the missing gaps. Memories are important, because they are part of what makes you different from everyone else. No one else will remember the same things in the same way as you do.

Memories are stored away in your brain,

You can bring them out again and again.

Believe me, when you're old and gray,

What you remember will make your day.

Day 1	3 months	8 months	14 months
I was born.	Mandy, our dog, came to live with us.	My first words were Dada and boo boo. I have no idea what that meant. Mandy ate my teddy bear.	I learned to walk.

6½ years — Grandpa died. Mom was very sad. It made me sad.

7 years — I started primary school. I made lots of new friends. But Julia went to a different school and that made me sad.

A timeline of your life

To help you make the most of your memories, you can make a time line. This is a simple diagram of your life with the dates when you started school, moved, or got your pets. Try to remember how you felt about the events at the time. There may have been some major events in your life that made you sad and some that made you smile. Try to put your feelings into your diagram too.

3 years   4½ years   5 years   6 years

I started nursery school. I met my friend, Julia.

I fell off the swing.

Grandma and Grandpa came from Canada to spend Christmas with us. Mandy ate the apple pie.

We went for a vacation at the beach. Dad fell off a fishing boat. Mandy ate a pail and a beach ball, but not all on the same day.

7½ years

I got a Game Boy for Christmas! Yes! Yes! Yes! I also got an ugly green ghost outfit from Grandma, but I lost it a day later.

Mandy had stomach ache. The vet said she had eaten something that disagreed with her. I wonder what it could have been?

19

My talents . . . .

Everyone is good at something. If everyone was good at the same things, just think how boring life would be! People who have different skills can get together and help each other. Everyone's contribution is equally important.

What are you good at?

Write a list of all the things you are good at. You don't just have to put down school work or sports. Some people have special talents for making friends, looking after animals, making great birthday cards, inventing fun games, or telling jokes. Those talents are just as important as being good at math or music or football.

Putting on a show

... so we're going to enter two groups in the competition. Phoebe, dear, why don't you select the people you want for your group first.

She'll pick all the best actors in the class and leave us with nobody. I can't believe Ms. Stewart lets her get away with it!

So I'll take the lead part, and everybody else must have parts too, because we're all so good.

Shouldn't someone sort out costumes, lights, and props and all that boring stuff?

Well, we've got two good actors, and if we rearrange the action a bit, use a narrator and play some moody music, Jane and I can take all the speaking parts on stage.

Someone turn the lights on!

Phew! I'll be in charge of costumes, Max. I'm good at sewing.

I'll do the sound effects and lights, I'm good at electronics.

I'll be the narrator, I'm good at reading.

Who's going to pull the curtain? Are we having music?

I do think someone should have organized some costumes.

Bravo! Bravo! More! Well done!

Well, Phoebe, your group's performance was certainly interesting. It was a pity the stage was in darkness and that some of you had to shout from behind the curtain. I wasn't terribly convinced by kings and queens and knights wearing jeans and T-shirts. Somehow the piece lacked... drama!

And the well-deserved first prize is yours! Beautifully staged! Everything added to the atmosphere – the lights, costumes, music... Enchanting! Excellent teamwork! Well done everyone!

Now listen here, and catch my drift,

Everyone's got some special gift,

Something they do that's better than most,

We've all got some good reason to boast!

My life . . . .

What kind of a life are you going to have? Do you think there is any way of knowing in advance? Is it all about luck, or do you think the choices you make may have something to do with it?

See the future now!

You will become a dentist... or maybe you will visit a dentist... very soon, my dear, very soon...

Ah! ha! ha! ha! ha! I see a circus clown in your future... and a troupe of dancing dogs...

You will marry a dark-haired man... or maybe a fair-haired one... perhaps a red-head...

Be yourself!

There is no real way of telling what will happen to us in the future. But there is one thing you can be sure of. You can make a difference in your life. If you choose the right friends, make the most of your talents, and think for yourself, then you are well on the way to a happy life.

Peer pressure

Do you choose fashions just because everyone else is following that style?

Do you just go along with things because everybody else does?

If everybody suggested doing something that you thought was wrong, would you stand up and say what you feel?

You can decide what your life will be,

Joyful and happy or as sad as can be.

Be your own person, don't go with the crowd.

"I'm ME – I'm SPECIAL!" Yeah! Shout it out loud!

Recipe for a happy life . .

Everyone would like a happy life. Every life is completely different from the next, but they all have the same basic ingredients. So let's get baking...

The first and most important ingredient is YOU!
You, with all your special talents and gifts. To make this ingredient work well, you must be sure to make the best of those talents.

The next ingredient is LOVE.
Every life recipe needs a lot of this. It comes from families and friends. Love, laughter, and friendship make people happy.

Next comes KNOWING.
This is a complicated ingredient, but a very important one. It means knowing who you are, and knowing who your real friends are. It means not kidding yourself!

Then LIFE comes along and mixes all the ingredients up a bit...

The final ingredient is DOING. It's important to try to do your best at school. Get busy with a hobby or a sport. Do something nice for someone else. And most important, take good care of yourself!

It takes time to bake it, of course...

And there's your happy life! It doesn't matter what it looks like, or if it's big or small. If you start with good ingredients, it will always taste good, even if it looks a bit funny.

It's been fun spending time with you,

Now brothers and sisters, here's what to do:

Think for yourself, life's all about living.

Don't tell yourself lies, be loving and giving.

LETTER FROM LIFE EDUCATION

Dear Friends:

The first Life Education Center was opened in Sydney, Australia, in 1979. Founded by the Rev. Ted Noffs, the Life Education program came about as a result of his many years of work with drug addicts and their families. Noffs realized that preventive education, beginning with children from the earliest possible age all the way into their teenage years, was the only long-term solution to drug abuse and other related social problems.

Life Education pioneered the use of technology in a "Classroom of the 21st Century," designed to show how drugs, including nicotine and alcohol, can destroy the delicate balance of human life. In every Life Education classroom, electronic displays show the major body systems, including the respiratory, nervous, digestive and immune systems. There is also a talking brain, a wondrous star ceiling, and Harold the Giraffe, Life Education's official mascot. Programs start in preschool and continue through high school.

Life Education also conducts parents' programs including violence prevention classes, and it has also begun to create interactive software for home and school computers.

There are Life Education Centers operating in seven countries (Thailand, the United States, the United Kingdom, New Zealand, Australia, Hong Kong, and New Guinea), and there is a Life Education home page on the Internet (the address is http://www.lec.org/).

If you would like to learn more about Life Education International contact us at one of the addresses listed below or, if you have a computer with a modem, you can write to Harold the Giraffe at Harold@lec.org and you'll find out that a giraffe can send E-mail!

Let's learn to live.

All of us at the Life Education Center.

Life Education, USA
149 Addison Ave
Elmhurst, Illinois
60126
USA
Tel: 630 530 8999
Fax: 630 530 7241

Life Education, UK
20 Long Lane
London
EC1A 9HL
United Kingdom
Tel: 0171 600 6969
Fax: 0171 600 6979

Life Education,
Australia
PO Box 1671
Potts Point
NSW 2011
Australia
Tel: 0061 2 358 2466
Fax: 0061 2 357 2569

Life Education,
New Zealand
126 The Terrace
PO Box 10-769
Wellington
New Zealand
Tel: 0064 4 472 9620
Fax: 0064 4 472 9609

Useful words

Achieve To manage to do things in your life, for example, to learn how to play football, or to make good friends.

Contribution The part you take when you play, work, or talk with other people. *Your* contribution is made up of all the things *you* do in the group.

Events The important things that have happened in your life. For example, the first day you went to school, the year you learned to swim, or the day your baby brother or sister (if you have either of these!) was born.

Experiences All the things you have seen, heard, read about, or felt in your life. Some experiences may make you feel happy; others may make you sad.

Identical Exactly the same as something else. Identical twins look exactly the same.

Memories All the things you remember from your past. Memories can make you smile, laugh, cringe, or cry!

Opinions The ideas you hold about certain things. You may not always agree with everybody else's opinions, and they may not always agree with yours.

Personality The type of character that a person has. He or she may have a chatty, quiet, shy, or caring personality – or their personality may be a mixture all of these things.

Talents The things you are especially good at. For example, listening to people, playing the guitar, doing math, and so on.

Index

Useful addresses

Character Education Institute
8918 Tesoro Drive, Suite 575
San Antonio, TX 78217
Telephone: 210-829-1727
Toll-free: 800-284-0499
Fax: 210-829-1729

Junior Optimist Clubs
4494 Lindell Boulevard
St. Louis, MO 63108
Telephone: 314-371-6000
Fax: 314-371-6006

Key Club International
3636 Woodview Trace
Indianapolis, IN 46268
Telephone: 317-875-8755

Quest International
P.O. Box 566
Granville, OH 43023
Telephone: 614-522-6400
Toll-free: 800-446-2700
Fax: 614-522-6580

U.S. Junior Chamber of
Commerce
P.O. Box 7
4 West 21st Street
Tulsa, OK 74102
Telephone: 918-584-2481
Fax: 918-582-7736

Youth Service America
1101 15th Street W., Suite 200
Washington, DC 20004
Telephone: 202-296-2992